Love Yourself First

102 Quotes For Discovering Self-Love Everyday

By Erica Carter

Love Yourself First

102 Quotes For Discovering Self-Love Everyday

By Erica Carter

Printed by Amazon KDP
Created and published through the Publishing to Profit Training Quote Book
Generator

Introduction

There are so many days you wake up and don't quite feel the best. When you wake up feeling that way, you may have some negative self-talk going on either in your head or out loud. This book will allow you to take just a few minutes throughout your day to change your self-talk!.

When you speak to your self positively, you absolutely love yourself. This is because you love the positivity that you are getting inside and out.

Within these pages are noteworthy quotes to help you to reflect and love yourself more and more each day. I want to personally congratulate you for beginning this journey of self-love, deeper understanding of yourself, and reflection of the language you use with yourself.

Enjoy the process, you are worth it!

"Self-love has very little to do with how you feel about your outer self. It's about accepting all of yourself." -Tyra Banks

Beginning Your Day

What does this quote mean to me personally today?

____
____
____

How will I apply this quote today?

____
____
____

Who else needs to hear this quote today?

____
____

At the End of Your Day

How did I apply this quote today?

____
____
____

What will I do differently going forward?

____
____
____

"Our deepest fear is not that we are inadequate. It is that we are powerful beyond our measure. It is our light, not our darkness that most frightens us. We ask ourselves, 'Who am I to be brilliant, gorgeous, talented, fabulous?' Actually, who are you not to be? Your playing small does not serve the world. There is nothing enlightened about shrinking so that other people won't feel insecure around you." -Marianne Williamson

Beginning Your Day

What does this quote mean to me personally today?

____

____

____

How will I apply this quote today?

____

____

____

Who else needs to hear this quote today?

____

____

____

At the End of Your Day

How did I apply this quote today?

____

____

____

What will I do differently going forward?

____

____

____

"Do your thing and don't care if they like it."
-Tina Fey

Beginning Your Day

What does this quote mean to me personally today?

____

____

____

How will I apply this quote today?

____

____

____

Who else needs to hear this quote today?

____

____

____

At the End of Your Day

How did I apply this quote today?

____

____

____

What will I do differently going forward?

____

____

____

"As you become more clear about who you really are, you'll be better able to decide what is best for you - the first time around." -Oprah Winfrey

Beginning Your Day

What does this quote mean to me personally today?

____

____

____

How will I apply this quote today?

____

____

____

Who else needs to hear this quote today?

____

____

____

At the End of Your Day

How did I apply this quote today?

____

____

____

What will I do differently going forward?

____

____

____

"No one can make you feel inferior without your consent." -Eleanor Roosevelt

Beginning Your Day

What does this quote mean to me personally today?

____

____

____

How will I apply this quote today?

____

____

____

Who else needs to hear this quote today?

____

____

____

At the End of Your Day

How did I apply this quote today?

____

____

____

What will I do differently going forward?

____

____

____

"I will not let anyone walk through my mind with their dirty feet" -Mahatma Gandhi

Beginning Your Day

What does this quote mean to me personally today?

____
____
____

How will I apply this quote today?

____
____
____

Who else needs to hear this quote today?

____
____
____

At the End of Your Day

How did I apply this quote today?

____
____
____

What will I do differently going forward?

____
____
____

"Your time is limited, so don't waste it living someone else's life." -Steve Jobs

Beginning Your Day

What does this quote mean to me personally today?

____

____

____

How will I apply this quote today?

____

____

____

Who else needs to hear this quote today?

____

____

____

At the End of Your Day

How did I apply this quote today?

____

____

____

What will I do differently going forward?

____

____

____

"It's not the absence of fear. It's overcoming it." -Emma Watson

Beginning Your Day

What does this quote mean to me personally today?

____

____

____

How will I apply this quote today?

____

____

____

Who else needs to hear this quote today?

____

____

____

At the End of Your Day

How did I apply this quote today?

____

____

____

What will I do differently going forward?

____

____

____

"If you are silent about your pain, they'll kill you and say you enjoyed it." -Zora Neale Hurston

Beginning Your Day

What does this quote mean to me personally today?

____

____

____

How will I apply this quote today?

____

____

____

Who else needs to hear this quote today?

____

____

____

At the End of Your Day

How did I apply this quote today?

____

____

____

What will I do differently going forward?

____

____

____

"Your self-worth is determined by you. You don't have to depend on someone telling you who you are." -Beyonce

Beginning Your Day

What does this quote mean to me personally today?

____

____

____

How will I apply this quote today?

____

____

____

Who else needs to hear this quote today?

____

____

____

At the End of Your Day

How did I apply this quote today?

____

____

____

What will I do differently going forward?

____

____

____

"Self-love know no impediment." -Linda Obst

Beginning Your Day

What does this quote mean to me personally today?

____

____

____

How will I apply this quote today?

____

____

____

Who else needs to hear this quote today?

____

____

____

At the End of Your Day

How did I apply this quote today?

____

____

____

What will I do differently going forward?

____

____

____

**"Look up at the stars and not down at your feet. Try to make sense of what you see, and wonder about what makes the universe exist. Be curious."
-Stephen Hawking**

Beginning Your Day
What does this quote mean to me personally today?

How will I apply this quote today?

Who else needs to hear this quote today?

At the End of Your Day
How did I apply this quote today?

What will I do differently going forward?

"Never make someone a priority when all you are to them is an option." -Maya Angelou

Beginning Your Day

What does this quote mean to me personally today?

____
____
____

How will I apply this quote today?

____
____
____

Who else needs to hear this quote today?

____
____
____

At the End of Your Day

How did I apply this quote today?

____
____
____

What will I do differently going forward?

____
____
____

"Love your enemies, for they tell you your faults." -Benjamin Franklin

Beginning Your Day

What does this quote mean to me personally today?

____

____

____

How will I apply this quote today?

____

____

____

Who else needs to hear this quote today?

____

____

____

At the End of Your Day

How did I apply this quote today?

____

____

____

What will I do differently going forward?

____

____

____

"Dare to love yourself as if you were a rainbow with gold at both ends." -Aberjhani

Beginning Your Day

What does this quote mean to me personally today?

____

____

____

How will I apply this quote today?

____

____

____

Who else needs to hear this quote today?

____

____

____

At the End of Your Day

How did I apply this quote today?

____

____

____

What will I do differently going forward?

____

____

____

"Love yourself first, because that's who you'll be spending the rest of your life with." -Erica Carter

Beginning Your Day

What does this quote mean to me personally today?

____

____

____

How will I apply this quote today?

____

____

____

Who else needs to hear this quote today?

____

____

____

At the End of Your Day

How did I apply this quote today?

____

____

____

What will I do differently going forward?

____

____

____

"In order to love who you are, you cannot hate the experiences that shape you." -Andrea Dykstra

Beginning Your Day

What does this quote mean to me personally today?

____

____

____

How will I apply this quote today?

____

____

____

Who else needs to hear this quote today?

____

____

____

At the End of Your Day

How did I apply this quote today?

____

____

____

What will I do differently going forward?

____

____

____

"Surround yourself with people who want nothing from you... and then give them everything." -Jeff Hood

Beginning Your Day

What does this quote mean to me personally today?

____

____

____

How will I apply this quote today?

____

____

____

Who else needs to hear this quote today?

____

____

____

At the End of Your Day

How did I apply this quote today?

____

____

____

What will I do differently going forward?

____

____

____

"You cannot consistently perform in a manner which is inconsistent with the way you see yourself." -Zig Ziglar

Beginning Your Day

What does this quote mean to me personally today?

____

____

____

How will I apply this quote today?

____

____

____

Who else needs to hear this quote today?

____

____

____

At the End of Your Day

How did I apply this quote today?

____

____

____

What will I do differently going forward?

____

____

____

"A seed planted in the ground does not feel its lack of roots, stem and petals as a 'weakness' or being 'less than'. It simply sees an opportunity to grow and then does." -Michael Stevenson

Beginning Your Day

What does this quote mean to me personally today?

____

____

____

How will I apply this quote today?

____

____

____

Who else needs to hear this quote today?

____

____

____

At the End of Your Day

How did I apply this quote today?

____

____

____

What will I do differently going forward?

____

____

____

"Self-love isn't selfish; You cannot truly love another until you know how to love yourself." -

Beginning Your Day

What does this quote mean to me personally today?

____

____

____

How will I apply this quote today?

____

____

____

Who else needs to hear this quote today?

____

____

____

At the End of Your Day

How did I apply this quote today?

____

____

____

What will I do differently going forward?

____

____

____

"Don't change so people will like you. Be yourself and the right people will love the real you." -

Beginning Your Day

What does this quote mean to me personally today?

____

____

____

How will I apply this quote today?

____

____

____

Who else needs to hear this quote today?

____

____

____

At the End of Your Day

How did I apply this quote today?

____

____

____

What will I do differently going forward?

____

____

____

"Beauty begins the moment you decided to be yourself." -Coco Chanel

Beginning Your Day

What does this quote mean to me personally today?

____

____

____

How will I apply this quote today?

____

____

____

Who else needs to hear this quote today?

____

____

____

At the End of Your Day

How did I apply this quote today?

____

____

____

What will I do differently going forward?

____

____

____

"When saying 'yes' to others, make sure you aren't saying 'no' to yourself." -Paulo Coehlo

Beginning Your Day

What does this quote mean to me personally today?

____

____

____

How will I apply this quote today?

____

____

____

Who else needs to hear this quote today?

____

____

____

At the End of Your Day

How did I apply this quote today?

____

____

____

What will I do differently going forward?

____

____

____

"Think like a queen. A queen is not afraid to fail. Failure is another stepping stone to greatness." -Oprah Winfrey

Beginning Your Day

What does this quote mean to me personally today?

____

____

____

How will I apply this quote today?

____

____

____

Who else needs to hear this quote today?

____

____

____

At the End of Your Day

How did I apply this quote today?

____

____

____

What will I do differently going forward?

____

____

____

"I can't change the direction of the wind, but I can adjust my sails to always reach my destination." -Jimmy Dean

Beginning Your Day
What does this quote mean to me personally today?

____

____

____

How will I apply this quote today?

____

____

____

Who else needs to hear this quote today?

____

____

____

At the End of Your Day
How did I apply this quote today?

____

____

____

What will I do differently going forward?

____

____

____

"You yourself, as much as anybody in the entire universe, deserve your love and affection."
-Buddha

Beginning Your Day

What does this quote mean to me personally today?

____

____

____

How will I apply this quote today?

____

____

____

Who else needs to hear this quote today?

____

____

____

At the End of Your Day

How did I apply this quote today?

____

____

____

What will I do differently going forward?

____

____

____

"Let us always meet each other with a smile, for the smile is the beginning of love." -Mother Teresa

Beginning Your Day

What does this quote mean to me personally today?

____

____

____

How will I apply this quote today?

____

____

____

Who else needs to hear this quote today?

____

____

____

At the End of Your Day

How did I apply this quote today?

____

____

____

What will I do differently going forward?

____

____

____

"it is not the mountain we conquer but ourselves."
-Sir Edmund Hillary

Beginning Your Day

What does this quote mean to me personally today?

____

____

____

How will I apply this quote today?

____

____

____

Who else needs to hear this quote today?

____

____

____

At the End of Your Day

How did I apply this quote today?

____

____

____

What will I do differently going forward?

____

____

____

"Your journey has molded you for your greater good, and it was exactly what it needed to be. Don't think that you've lost time. It took each and every situation you have encountered to bring you to the now. And now is right on time." -Asha Tyson

Beginning Your Day

What does this quote mean to me personally today?

____

____

____

How will I apply this quote today?

____

____

____

Who else needs to hear this quote today?

____

____

____

At the End of Your Day

How did I apply this quote today?

____

____

____

What will I do differently going forward?

____

____

____

"Sometimes you have to be alone to truly know you're worth." -Karen A Baquiran

Beginning Your Day

What does this quote mean to me personally today?

____

____

____

How will I apply this quote today?

____

____

____

Who else needs to hear this quote today?

____

____

____

At the End of Your Day

How did I apply this quote today?

____

____

____

What will I do differently going forward?

____

____

____

"You can't have a better tomorrow if you are always thinking about yesterday." -Charles F. Kettering

Beginning Your Day

What does this quote mean to me personally today?

____

____

____

How will I apply this quote today?

____

____

____

Who else needs to hear this quote today?

____

____

____

At the End of Your Day

How did I apply this quote today?

____

____

____

What will I do differently going forward?

____

____

____

"You've got to learn to leave the table with love's no longer being served." -Nina Simone

Beginning Your Day

What does this quote mean to me personally today?

____

____

____

How will I apply this quote today?

____

____

____

Who else needs to hear this quote today?

____

____

____

At the End of Your Day

How did I apply this quote today?

____

____

____

What will I do differently going forward?

____

____

____

"Good, better, best. Never let it rest, until the good is better and the better is best." -Erica Carter

Beginning Your Day

What does this quote mean to me personally today?

____
____
____

How will I apply this quote today?

____
____
____

Who else needs to hear this quote today?

____
____
____

At the End of Your Day

How did I apply this quote today?

____
____
____

What will I do differently going forward?

____
____
____

"There are people who dislike you because you do not dislike yourself." -

Beginning Your Day

What does this quote mean to me personally today?

____

____

____

How will I apply this quote today?

____

____

____

Who else needs to hear this quote today?

____

____

____

At the End of Your Day

How did I apply this quote today?

____

____

____

What will I do differently going forward?

____

____

____

"If it scares you, it might be a good thing to try." -Seth Godin

Beginning Your Day

What does this quote mean to me personally today?

____

____

____

How will I apply this quote today?

____

____

____

Who else needs to hear this quote today?

____

____

____

At the End of Your Day

How did I apply this quote today?

____

____

____

What will I do differently going forward?

____

____

____

"The measure of who we are is what we do with what we have." -Vince Lombardi

Beginning Your Day

What does this quote mean to me personally today?

____

____

____

How will I apply this quote today?

____

____

____

Who else needs to hear this quote today?

____

____

____

At the End of Your Day

How did I apply this quote today?

____

____

____

What will I do differently going forward?

____

____

____

"People are weird. When we find someone with weirdness that is compatible with ours, we team up and call it love." -Dr. Seuss

Beginning Your Day

What does this quote mean to me personally today?

____

____

____

How will I apply this quote today?

____

____

____

Who else needs to hear this quote today?

____

____

____

At the End of Your Day

How did I apply this quote today?

____

____

____

What will I do differently going forward?

____

____

____

"Self-love seems so often unrequited." -Anthony Powell

Beginning Your Day

What does this quote mean to me personally today?

____

____

____

How will I apply this quote today?

____

____

____

Who else needs to hear this quote today?

____

____

____

At the End of Your Day

How did I apply this quote today?

____

____

____

What will I do differently going forward?

____

____

____

"It's not selfish to love yourself, take care of yourself and to make your happiness a priority. It's necessary." -Mandy Hale

Beginning Your Day
What does this quote mean to me personally today?

____

____

____

How will I apply this quote today?

____

____

____

Who else needs to hear this quote today?

____

____

____

At the End of Your Day
How did I apply this quote today?

____

____

____

What will I do differently going forward?

____

____

____

"If you hear a voice within you say 'you cannot paint,' then by all means, paint, and that voice will be silenced." -Vincent Van Gogh

Beginning Your Day

What does this quote mean to me personally today?

____

____

____

How will I apply this quote today?

____

____

____

Who else needs to hear this quote today?

____

____

____

At the End of Your Day

How did I apply this quote today?

____

____

____

What will I do differently going forward?

____

____

____

"Well-ordered self-love is right and natural."
-Thomas Aquinas

Beginning Your Day

What does this quote mean to me personally today?

____
____
____

How will I apply this quote today?

____
____
____

Who else needs to hear this quote today?

____
____
____

At the End of Your Day

How did I apply this quote today?

____
____
____

What will I do differently going forward?

____
____
____

"I'd rather regret the things I've done, than regret the things I haven't done." -Lucille Ball

Beginning Your Day

What does this quote mean to me personally today?

____

____

____

How will I apply this quote today?

____

____

____

Who else needs to hear this quote today?

____

____

____

At the End of Your Day

How did I apply this quote today?

____

____

____

What will I do differently going forward?

____

____

____

"Self-love is often rather arrogant than blind; It does not hide our faults from ourselves, but persuades us that they escape the notice of others." -Samuel Johnson

Beginning Your Day

What does this quote mean to me personally today?

____

____

____

How will I apply this quote today?

____

____

____

Who else needs to hear this quote today?

____

____

____

At the End of Your Day

How did I apply this quote today?

____

____

____

What will I do differently going forward?

____

____

____

"We cannot hold a torch to light another's path without brightening our own." -Ben Sweetland

Beginning Your Day

What does this quote mean to me personally today?

____

____

____

How will I apply this quote today?

____

____

____

Who else needs to hear this quote today?

____

____

____

At the End of Your Day

How did I apply this quote today?

____

____

____

What will I do differently going forward?

____

____

____

"Happiness is not something you postpone for the future; it is something you design for the present." -Jim Rohn

Beginning Your Day

What does this quote mean to me personally today?

____

____

____

How will I apply this quote today?

____

____

____

Who else needs to hear this quote today?

____

____

____

At the End of Your Day

How did I apply this quote today?

____

____

____

What will I do differently going forward?

____

____

____

"The purpose of art is washing the dust of daily life off our souls." -Pablo Picasso

Beginning Your Day

What does this quote mean to me personally today?

____

____

____

How will I apply this quote today?

____

____

____

Who else needs to hear this quote today?

____

____

____

At the End of Your Day

How did I apply this quote today?

____

____

____

What will I do differently going forward?

____

____

____

"The secret of change is to focus all of your energy not on fighting the old, but on building the new." -Socrates

Beginning Your Day

What does this quote mean to me personally today?

____

____

____

How will I apply this quote today?

____

____

____

Who else needs to hear this quote today?

____

____

____

At the End of Your Day

How did I apply this quote today?

____

____

____

What will I do differently going forward?

____

____

____

"Be yourself; everyone else is already taken."
-Oscar Wilde

Beginning Your Day

What does this quote mean to me personally today?

____

____

____

How will I apply this quote today?

____

____

____

Who else needs to hear this quote today?

____

____

____

At the End of Your Day

How did I apply this quote today?

____

____

____

What will I do differently going forward?

____

____

____

"I'm not extraordinary. I'm simply an ordinary woman who chooses every day to make extraordinary decisions." -Lisa Nichols

Beginning Your Day

What does this quote mean to me personally today?

____

____

____

How will I apply this quote today?

____

____

____

Who else needs to hear this quote today?

____

____

____

At the End of Your Day

How did I apply this quote today?

____

____

____

What will I do differently going forward?

____

____

____

"Take care how you speak to yourself because you are listening." -Lisa M. Hayes

Beginning Your Day

What does this quote mean to me personally today?

____

____

____

How will I apply this quote today?

____

____

____

Who else needs to hear this quote today?

____

____

____

At the End of Your Day

How did I apply this quote today?

____

____

____

What will I do differently going forward?

____

____

____

"Always know how valuable and uniquely beautiful you are." -

Beginning Your Day

What does this quote mean to me personally today?

____

____

____

How will I apply this quote today?

____

____

____

Who else needs to hear this quote today?

____

____

____

At the End of Your Day

How did I apply this quote today?

____

____

____

What will I do differently going forward?

____

____

____

"Find beauty in places where others have not dared to look including inside ourselves." -Selma Hayer

Beginning Your Day

What does this quote mean to me personally today?

____

____

____

How will I apply this quote today?

____

____

____

Who else needs to hear this quote today?

____

____

____

At the End of Your Day

How did I apply this quote today?

____

____

____

What will I do differently going forward?

____

____

____

"How you love yourself is how you teach others to love you." -Rupi Kaur

Beginning Your Day

What does this quote mean to me personally today?

____

____

____

How will I apply this quote today?

____

____

____

Who else needs to hear this quote today?

____

____

____

At the End of Your Day

How did I apply this quote today?

____

____

____

What will I do differently going forward?

____

____

____

"If you aren't in the moment, you are either looking forward to uncertainty, or back to pain and regret." -Jim Carrey

Beginning Your Day

What does this quote mean to me personally today?

____

____

____

How will I apply this quote today?

____

____

____

Who else needs to hear this quote today?

____

____

____

At the End of Your Day

How did I apply this quote today?

____

____

____

What will I do differently going forward?

____

____

____

"Before you diagnose yourself with depression or low self-esteem, first make sure you are not, in fact, surrounded by assholes." -Sigmund Freud

Beginning Your Day

What does this quote mean to me personally today?

____

____

____

How will I apply this quote today?

____

____

____

Who else needs to hear this quote today?

____

____

____

At the End of Your Day

How did I apply this quote today?

____

____

____

What will I do differently going forward?

____

____

____

"Sometimes if you want to see a change for the better, you have to take things into your own hands." -Clint Eastwood

Beginning Your Day

What does this quote mean to me personally today?

____

____

How will I apply this quote today?

____

____

Who else needs to hear this quote today?

____

____

At the End of Your Day

How did I apply this quote today?

____

____

What will I do differently going forward?

____

____

"Nothing is impossible, the word itself says 'I'm possible'!" -Audrey Hepburn

Beginning Your Day

What does this quote mean to me personally today?

____

____

____

How will I apply this quote today?

____

____

____

Who else needs to hear this quote today?

____

____

____

At the End of Your Day

How did I apply this quote today?

____

____

____

What will I do differently going forward?

____

____

____

"Love yourself first and everything else falls into line." -Lucille Ball

Beginning Your Day

What does this quote mean to me personally today?

____

____

____

How will I apply this quote today?

____

____

____

Who else needs to hear this quote today?

____

____

____

At the End of Your Day

How did I apply this quote today?

____

____

____

What will I do differently going forward?

____

____

____

"If your actions inspire others to dream more, learn more, do more and become more, you are a leader." -John Quincy Adams

Beginning Your Day

What does this quote mean to me personally today?

____

____

____

How will I apply this quote today?

____

____

____

Who else needs to hear this quote today?

____

____

____

At the End of Your Day

How did I apply this quote today?

____

____

____

What will I do differently going forward?

____

____

____

"Loving ourselves works miracles in our lives." -Louise L Hay

Beginning Your Day
What does this quote mean to me personally today?

____

____

____

How will I apply this quote today?

____

____

____

Who else needs to hear this quote today?

____

____

____

At the End of Your Day
How did I apply this quote today?

____

____

____

What will I do differently going forward?

____

____

____

"Kindness is loving yourself enough to love those around you." -RAK Twist

Beginning Your Day

What does this quote mean to me personally today?

____

____

____

How will I apply this quote today?

____

____

____

Who else needs to hear this quote today?

____

____

____

At the End of Your Day

How did I apply this quote today?

____

____

____

What will I do differently going forward?

____

____

____

"Your task is not to seek for love, but merely to seek and find all the barriers within yourself that you have built against it." -Rumi

Beginning Your Day

What does this quote mean to me personally today?

____

____

____

How will I apply this quote today?

____

____

____

Who else needs to hear this quote today?

____

____

____

At the End of Your Day

How did I apply this quote today?

____

____

____

What will I do differently going forward?

____

____

____

"We often fancy that we suffer ingratitude, while in reality we suffer from self-love." -Walter Savage London

Beginning Your Day

What does this quote mean to me personally today?

____
____
____

How will I apply this quote today?

____
____
____

Who else needs to hear this quote today?

____
____
____

At the End of Your Day

How did I apply this quote today?

____
____
____

What will I do differently going forward?

____
____
____

"If you don't love yourself, nobody will. Not only that, you won't be good at loving anyone else. Loving starts with the self. " -Wayne Dyer

Beginning Your Day

What does this quote mean to me personally today?

____

____

____

How will I apply this quote today?

____

____

____

Who else needs to hear this quote today?

____

____

____

At the End of Your Day

How did I apply this quote today?

____

____

____

What will I do differently going forward?

____

____

____

"To fall in love with yourself is the first secret to happiness." -Robert Morley

Beginning Your Day

What does this quote mean to me personally today?

____

____

____

How will I apply this quote today?

____

____

____

Who else needs to hear this quote today?

____

____

____

At the End of Your Day

How did I apply this quote today?

____

____

____

What will I do differently going forward?

____

____

____

"I am only one, but, I am one. I cannot do everything, but, I can do something, and I will not let what I cannot do interfere with what I can do."
-Edward Everett Hale

Beginning Your Day
What does this quote mean to me personally today?

____

____

____

How will I apply this quote today?

____

____

____

Who else needs to hear this quote today?

____

____

____

At the End of Your Day
How did I apply this quote today?

____

____

____

What will I do differently going forward?

____

____

____

"You're going to go through tough times ? that's life. But I say, 'Nothing happens to you, it happens for you.' See the positive in negative events." -Joel Osteen

Beginning Your Day
What does this quote mean to me personally today?

____

____

____

How will I apply this quote today?

____

____

____

Who else needs to hear this quote today?

____

____

____

At the End of Your Day
How did I apply this quote today?

____

____

____

What will I do differently going forward?

____

____

____

"To know oneself, one should assert oneself."
-Albert Camus

Beginning Your Day

What does this quote mean to me personally today?

____

____

____

How will I apply this quote today?

____

____

____

Who else needs to hear this quote today?

____

____

____

At the End of Your Day

How did I apply this quote today?

____

____

____

What will I do differently going forward?

____

____

____

"I do not care so much what I am to others as I care what I am to myself." -Michael De Montaigne

Beginning Your Day

What does this quote mean to me personally today?

____

____

____

How will I apply this quote today?

____

____

____

Who else needs to hear this quote today?

____

____

____

At the End of Your Day

How did I apply this quote today?

____

____

____

What will I do differently going forward?

____

____

____

"Do you love yourself enough to be what you love yourself enough to want?" -Stee Maraboli

Beginning Your Day

What does this quote mean to me personally today?

____

____

____

How will I apply this quote today?

____

____

____

Who else needs to hear this quote today?

____

____

____

At the End of Your Day

How did I apply this quote today?

____

____

____

What will I do differently going forward?

____

____

____

"Be not afraid of growing slowly, be afraid only of standing still." -Chinese Proverb

Beginning Your Day

What does this quote mean to me personally today?

How will I apply this quote today?

Who else needs to hear this quote today?

At the End of Your Day

How did I apply this quote today?

What will I do differently going forward?

"We can learn something new anytime we believe we can." -Virginia Satir

Beginning Your Day

What does this quote mean to me personally today?

____

____

How will I apply this quote today?

____

____

Who else needs to hear this quote today?

____

____

At the End of Your Day

How did I apply this quote today?

____

____

What will I do differently going forward?

____

____

"A wise man can learn more from a foolish question than a fool can learn from a wise answer." -Bruce Lee

Beginning Your Day

What does this quote mean to me personally today?

____

____

____

How will I apply this quote today?

____

____

____

Who else needs to hear this quote today?

____

____

____

At the End of Your Day

How did I apply this quote today?

____

____

____

What will I do differently going forward?

____

____

____

"A man cannot be comfortable without his won approval." -Mark Twain

Beginning Your Day

What does this quote mean to me personally today?

____

____

____

How will I apply this quote today?

____

____

____

Who else needs to hear this quote today?

____

____

____

At the End of Your Day

How did I apply this quote today?

____

____

____

What will I do differently going forward?

____

____

____

"As long as we persevere and endure, we can get anything we want." -Mike Tyson

Beginning Your Day

What does this quote mean to me personally today?

____

____

____

How will I apply this quote today?

____

____

____

Who else needs to hear this quote today?

____

____

____

At the End of Your Day

How did I apply this quote today?

____

____

____

What will I do differently going forward?

____

____

____

"Become the most positive and enthusiastic person you know." -

Beginning Your Day

What does this quote mean to me personally today?

____

____

____

How will I apply this quote today?

____

____

____

Who else needs to hear this quote today?

____

____

____

At the End of Your Day

How did I apply this quote today?

____

____

____

What will I do differently going forward?

____

____

____

"Don't find fault, find a remedy." -Henry Ford

Beginning Your Day

What does this quote mean to me personally today?

____

____

____

How will I apply this quote today?

____

____

____

Who else needs to hear this quote today?

____

____

____

At the End of Your Day

How did I apply this quote today?

____

____

____

What will I do differently going forward?

____

____

____

"Your smile will give you a positive countenance that will make people feel comfortable around you." -Les Brown

Beginning Your Day

What does this quote mean to me personally today?

____

____

____

How will I apply this quote today?

____

____

____

Who else needs to hear this quote today?

____

____

____

At the End of Your Day

How did I apply this quote today?

____

____

____

What will I do differently going forward?

____

____

____

"Never settle being someone's OTHER when you have the potential to be someone's ONLY." -

Beginning Your Day
What does this quote mean to me personally today?

____

____

____

How will I apply this quote today?

____

____

____

Who else needs to hear this quote today?

____

____

____

At the End of Your Day
How did I apply this quote today?

____

____

____

What will I do differently going forward?

____

____

____

"Open your eyes, look within. Are you satisfied with the life you're living?" -Bob Marley

Beginning Your Day

What does this quote mean to me personally today?

____

____

____

How will I apply this quote today?

____

____

____

Who else needs to hear this quote today?

____

____

____

At the End of Your Day

How did I apply this quote today?

____

____

____

What will I do differently going forward?

____

____

____

"Wanting to be someone else is a wast of the person you are." -Marilyn Monroe

Beginning Your Day

What does this quote mean to me personally today?

____

____

____

How will I apply this quote today?

____

____

____

Who else needs to hear this quote today?

____

____

____

At the End of Your Day

How did I apply this quote today?

____

____

____

What will I do differently going forward?

____

____

____

"Loving yourself isn't vanity. It is sanity."
-Katrina Mayer

Beginning Your Day

What does this quote mean to me personally today?

____

____

____

How will I apply this quote today?

____

____

____

Who else needs to hear this quote today?

____

____

____

At the End of Your Day

How did I apply this quote today?

____

____

____

What will I do differently going forward?

____

____

____

"Keep your face to the sunshine and you cannot see a shadow." -Helen Keller

Beginning Your Day

What does this quote mean to me personally today?

____

____

____

How will I apply this quote today?

____

____

____

Who else needs to hear this quote today?

____

____

____

At the End of Your Day

How did I apply this quote today?

____

____

____

What will I do differently going forward?

____

____

____

"I have learned over the years that when one's mind is made up, that diminishes fear; knowing what must be done does away with fear." -Rosa Parks

Beginning Your Day

What does this quote mean to me personally today?

____

____

____

How will I apply this quote today?

____

____

____

Who else needs to hear this quote today?

____

____

____

At the End of Your Day

How did I apply this quote today?

____

____

____

What will I do differently going forward?

____

____

____

"Always put your best self forward, and keep a smile on your face, because you never know when someone is being encouraged by, or falling in love with your smile." -Kayla Moffett Stevenson

Beginning Your Day
What does this quote mean to me personally today?

____
____
____

How will I apply this quote today?

____
____
____

Who else needs to hear this quote today?

____
____
____

At the End of Your Day
How did I apply this quote today?

____
____
____

What will I do differently going forward?

____
____
____

"If you can dream it, you can do it." -Walt Disney

Beginning Your Day

What does this quote mean to me personally today?

____

____

____

How will I apply this quote today?

____

____

____

Who else needs to hear this quote today?

____

____

____

At the End of Your Day

How did I apply this quote today?

____

____

____

What will I do differently going forward?

____

____

____

"Be strong enough to stand alone, smart enough to know when you need help, and brave enough to ask for it." -Zaid K. Abdelnour

Beginning Your Day

What does this quote mean to me personally today?

____

____

____

How will I apply this quote today?

____

____

____

Who else needs to hear this quote today?

____

____

____

At the End of Your Day

How did I apply this quote today?

____

____

____

What will I do differently going forward?

____

____

____

"Work on being in love with the person in the mirror who has been through so much but is still standing." -Unknown

Beginning Your Day

What does this quote mean to me personally today?

____

____

____

How will I apply this quote today?

____

____

____

Who else needs to hear this quote today?

____

____

____

At the End of Your Day

How did I apply this quote today?

____

____

____

What will I do differently going forward?

____

____

____

"Had we not loved ourselves at all, we could never have been obliged to love anything. So that self-love is the basis of all love." -Thomas Traherne

Beginning Your Day

What does this quote mean to me personally today?

____

____

____

How will I apply this quote today?

____

____

____

Who else needs to hear this quote today?

____

____

____

At the End of Your Day

How did I apply this quote today?

____

____

____

What will I do differently going forward?

____

____

____

"If we are not a little bit uncomfortable every day, we're not growing. All the good stuff is outside our comfort zone." -Jack Canfield

Beginning Your Day

What does this quote mean to me personally today?

____

____

____

How will I apply this quote today?

____

____

____

Who else needs to hear this quote today?

____

____

____

At the End of Your Day

How did I apply this quote today?

____

____

____

What will I do differently going forward?

____

____

____

"Self respect, self worth and self love, all start with self. Stop looking outside of yourself for your value." -Rob Liano

Beginning Your Day

What does this quote mean to me personally today?

____

____

____

How will I apply this quote today?

____

____

____

Who else needs to hear this quote today?

____

____

____

At the End of Your Day

How did I apply this quote today?

____

____

____

What will I do differently going forward?

____

____

____

"Darkness cannot drive out darkness; only light can do that. Hate cannot drive out hate; only love can do that." -Martin Luther King, Jr.

Beginning Your Day

What does this quote mean to me personally today?

____

____

____

How will I apply this quote today?

____

____

____

Who else needs to hear this quote today?

____

____

____

At the End of Your Day

How did I apply this quote today?

____

____

____

What will I do differently going forward?

____

____

____

"When you practice gratefulness, there is a sense of respect toward others." -Dalai Lama

Beginning Your Day

What does this quote mean to me personally today?

____

____

____

How will I apply this quote today?

____

____

____

Who else needs to hear this quote today?

____

____

____

At the End of Your Day

How did I apply this quote today?

____

____

____

What will I do differently going forward?

____

____

____

"You carry so much love in your heart. Give some to yourself." -

Beginning Your Day

What does this quote mean to me personally today?

____

____

____

How will I apply this quote today?

____

____

____

Who else needs to hear this quote today?

____

____

____

At the End of Your Day

How did I apply this quote today?

____

____

____

What will I do differently going forward?

____

____

____

"Self-Love is your superpower" -Unknown

Beginning Your Day

What does this quote mean to me personally today?

____

____

____

How will I apply this quote today?

____

____

____

Who else needs to hear this quote today?

____

____

____

At the End of Your Day

How did I apply this quote today?

____

____

____

What will I do differently going forward?

____

____

____

"To love yourself right now, just as you are, is to give yourself heaven. Don't wait until you die. If you wait, you die now. If you love, you life now."
-Alan Cohen

Beginning Your Day

What does this quote mean to me personally today?

____

____

____

How will I apply this quote today?

____

____

____

Who else needs to hear this quote today?

____

____

____

At the End of Your Day

How did I apply this quote today?

____

____

____

What will I do differently going forward?

____

____

____

"It's not your job to like me - it's mine." -Byron Katie

Beginning Your Day
What does this quote mean to me personally today?

____

____

____

How will I apply this quote today?

____

____

____

Who else needs to hear this quote today?

____

____

____

At the End of Your Day
How did I apply this quote today?

____

____

____

What will I do differently going forward?

____

____

____

"You are not your mistakes; They are what you did, not who you are." -Lisa Lieberman-Wang

Beginning Your Day

What does this quote mean to me personally today?

____

____

____

How will I apply this quote today?

____

____

____

Who else needs to hear this quote today?

____

____

____

At the End of Your Day

How did I apply this quote today?

____

____

____

What will I do differently going forward?

____

____

____

"When I was 5 years old, my mother always told me that happiness was the key to life. When I went to school, they asked me what I wanted to be when I grew up. I wrote down 'happy'. They told me that I didn't understand the assignment, and I told them they didn't understand life." -John Lennon

Beginning Your Day

What does this quote mean to me personally today?

____
____
____

How will I apply this quote today?

____
____
____

Who else needs to hear this quote today?

____
____
____

At the End of Your Day

How did I apply this quote today?

____
____
____

What will I do differently going forward?

____
____
____

"Here's to the crazy ones, the misfits, the rebels, the troublemakers, the round pegs in the square holes, the ones who see things differently. They're not fond of rules. You can quote them, disagree with them, glorify or vilify them, but the only thing you can't do is ignore them because they change things? The ones who are crazy enough to think that they can change the world, are the ones who do." -Steve Jobs

Beginning Your Day

What does this quote mean to me personally today?

____

____

____

How will I apply this quote today?

____

____

____

Who else needs to hear this quote today?

____

____

____

At the End of Your Day

How did I apply this quote today?

____

____

____

What will I do differently going forward?

____

____

____

"You can't love anyone else, until you finally love who your are... inside and out." -Erica Carter

Beginning Your Day

What does this quote mean to me personally today?

How will I apply this quote today?

Who else needs to hear this quote today?

At the End of Your Day

How did I apply this quote today?

What will I do differently going forward?